SURREY

RAMBLES

Derek Palmer

With Historical Notes

COUNTRYSIDE BOOKS
NEWBURY, BERKSHIRE

First Published 1987
© Derek Palmer 1987
Revised Edition 1988

Updated and Reprinted 1990, 1991

COUNTRYSIDE BOOKS
3 Catherine Road
Newbury, Berkshire
ISBN 0 905392 77 9

Cover photograph is the North Downs at Newlands Corner
taken by the author
Sketch maps by Colin Redman
Produced through MRM (Print Consultants) Ltd., Reading
Typeset by Acorn Bookwork, Salisbury
Printed in England by J. W. Arrowsmith Ltd., Bristol

Contents

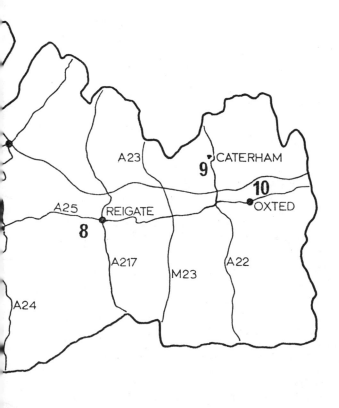

0 1 2 3 4 5 6 7 8 9 10

Miles

Introduction

It is an amazing fact that, right on the Londoner's doorstep, is the lovely walking countryside of Surrey, well within 30–60 minutes drive for millions of people. The walks in this book are intended to introduce you to some of the most attractive and popular features of this beautiful county. There is such a diversity of scenery waiting for you, with the clay heaths and commons, the chalk downlands, the wooded greensand hills, the very attractive farm and country houses and the quaint and historic villages. Running right across Surrey is part of a long-distance footpath – the North Downs Way, 140 miles in total length – which affords many magnificent views. Sections of it are traversed on some of the rambles.

The distance quoted for each walk is approximate, but accurate to within a quarter of a mile. An estimate of walking time is given, based on a reasonably good pace, so you should allow extra for stops if you are walking as a family.

The routes follow public footpaths, though bear in mind that changes in rights of way do occur from time to time. Remember, too, that it is always advisable to wear a strong pair of walking shoes or boots since you are likely to find the odd patch of mud, even in dry weather.

All of the routes are circular and the starting points have space for car parking. Details of public transport are given where appropriate but I strongly recommend checking with British Rail as many of the stations mentioned have an infrequent service on weekdays and none at all on Sundays. Bus routes are, of course, a little more complicated. Services are often even less frequent than the trains and sometimes run only one day of the week and mostly not at all on Sundays. In October 1986 Surrey County Council published comprehensive bus timetables. There are six of these books covering the whole county, and they are well worth the 10p cost of each. Refreshment possibilities are mentioned in an introductory paragraph to each walk.

Places of particular interest are indicated in the text by the initials HN and further information about them may be found in a special Historical Notes section at the end of each walk. I am indebted to John Janaway and his staff at the local studies library in Guildford for all the help they gave. Additionally, *The Surrey Village Book* by Graham Collyer of the *Surrey Advertiser*, was a wonderful source of information.

My thanks go to Colin Redman who drew the sketch maps. These provide a straightforward plan of the route to be followed. The numbers on the diagrams identify the numbered paragraphs in the text and are useful as an aid for checking your position. It is unnecessary to use proper maps, but for those who wish to do so, the numbers for the relevant Ordnance Survey Landranger and Pathfinder maps have been quoted. The grid reference relates to the starting point.

I would also like to thank members of the Surrey County Walkers who accompanied me on these rambles and made them especially enjoyable. I hope that you derive as much pleasure from your outings as we did.

Finally I wish to dedicate this book to my dear wife, Brenda, who helped me check and present the walks.

Derek Palmer
March 1991

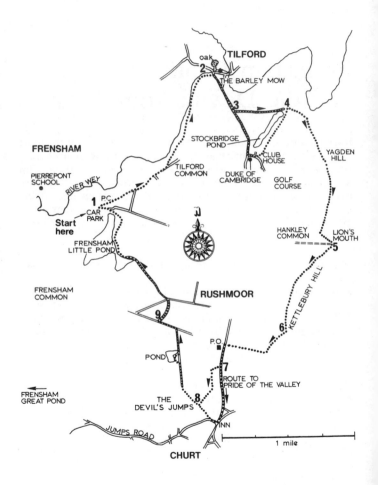

Frensham Ponds and the Devil's Jumps

Introduction: This is an attractive walk through one of the most picturesque and popular areas in Surrey. It commences near Frensham, well-known for its Great Pond, takes in Tilford with its historic green and, after passing Stockbridge Pond, continues over Yagden and Kettlebury Hills. The climb up one of the Devil's Jumps will then reward you with a panoramic view of the Hog's Back in one direction and parts of Hampshire and Sussex in the other.

Distance: This is a 7-mile circuit and will take around 3 hours.

Refreshments: Near the beginning of the walk is the Barley Mow inn at Tilford, but it does not serve meals. Another pub close to Tilford, The Duke of Cambridge, serves a limited range of hot food and may be reached by continuing down the road at Point 3. A useful stop for confectionery and ice cream is at the Post Office and Stores at Rushmoor.

How to get there: The walk commences from the large car park at Frensham Little Pond. Frensham is off the A287 south of Farnham. After entering the village of Frensham, you will pass Pierrepont School (HN) on the left. Opposite The Marriners inn on the right take a turning on the left signposted to Frensham Little Pond. In less than a mile you will pass the first car park on the right by a bend in the road. Continue another 200 yards to your car park which is also on the right and signposted 'Frensham Little Pond Car Park'. There is a bus service to Frensham, which is about a mile from the start of the walk. There is also a service to Tilford from where the walk can be joined at Point 2. (OS maps 186 or SU 84/94 & SU 83/93, GR 859418.)

The Walk:

1. Leave the car park by the entrance and turn right down the road. Soon you fork left on a wide track going in a north-easterly direction past public toilets. Stay on this track for half a mile. Bear left over a stile and later, just before a house, your path joins a wider track coming in from the right. When the path divides at a yellow waymark, branch left on a smaller path and shortly the river Wey will come into view. At a log seat bear slightly away from the river path to continue through the woods and go through a gate onto an enclosed path with a conifer nursery on your right. After passing a house on your left, bear left to a gate and you are at Tilford Green (HN).

2. Turn right on the road, leaving the green and then passing All Saints Church and continue along the road until you reach The Little House on your right.

3. If you wish to visit The Duke of Cambridge inn, continue down the road for nearly half a mile. After leaving the inn turn right on a track leading to Hankley Common Golf Club and, just before reaching the clubhouse, turn left across the car park to pick up a track leading from some posts. Continue along the side of the fairway, later going through woods to reach Stockbridge Pond (HN) on your left. At the end of the pond you turn right onto a track leading into a military training area.

3. If you do not wish to visit The Duke of Cambridge, turn left onto a track by a parking area, later reaching Stockbridge Pond (HN) on your right and, after passing the pond, continue direction to a military training area.

4. At a junction of three tracks, take the one on the right which soon becomes sunken. When you reach a more open area, continue ahead on the right fork and soon you will come to another fork where you bear right by a post. Continue over a crossing track on the side of Yagden Hill and at another junction of paths go straight ahead. You will soon come to a golf course on your right and, at a further junction of paths, you continue direction uphill. At the 11th tee turn left on a wide crossing track and, soon after reaching a fenced enclosure on your left, turn right steeply uphill on an even wider sandy track. This area is known as the Lion's Mouth.

5. At the top of Kettlebury Hill turn right on a fine ridge path. For almost a mile you will enjoy excellent views to the left and occasionally to the right over Hankley Common.

6. About 150 yards after passing a pill box on your left you will reach a wooden post. Here you should turn sharply right downhill, almost immediately bearing left to go over a crossing track in the valley below. Later your path bears right and you keep on it, ignoring turnings to the left and right, as it takes you steadily uphill. After going downhill again, you continue straight over a wide track running under telephone wires and over a stream to the road. Turn left, go past Rushmoor (HN) Post Office & Stores and cross Sandy Lane.

7. If you wish to visit The Pride of The Valley at Churt (HN), continue down the road for about half a mile and, after passing a road turning left, you will soon be at the inn. Leaving the inn, turn left down Jumps Road and, in about 100 yards, turn right onto a signposted footpath. This enclosed path leads you through the woods and later you bear slightly left to continue uphill on a stepped path taking you to the top of one of the Devil's Jumps (HN).

7. If you do not wish to visit the inn, turn right onto a footpath and, on reaching a junction of paths, turn left past the backs of some houses. Where the path divides go right and then fork right again towards some steps taking you to the top of the Devil's Jumps (HN).

8. Facing away from the stony crags and with a pond in view ahead and Frensham Common diagonally left, continue steeply downhill on a stepped path. At the bottom go over a crossing track and, at a junction of paths, turn left off the main track towards the pond. Turn right and continue round the edge of the pond, later bearing left over a planked bridge onto your original track. This will lead you to a road on which you turn left for about 250 yards.

9. Turn right onto a track next to the drive to Firwood. At the end of this, turn left onto an enclosed path with some old nissen huts on your right and go through a barrier. Continue on this path for a third of a mile and later bear left onto a smaller path by the side of Frensham Little Pond (HN). Keep on this path, close to the lake, which will eventually take you over a planked bridge by a sluice gate. Go through a barrier and bear left past the end of the lake, continuing along the road to reach the car park.

Historical Notes

Pierrepont School was a private house before the last war; it was owned by the Combe family who were members of the Watney brewing concern.

Frensham Great Pond is an enlarged natural pool, now almost two miles in circumference. As long ago as 1208 the pond was providing fish for the table of the Bishop of Winchester at Farnham Castle. The first seaplane was tested here in 1913. The depth of the pond varies considerably along its shore. Visitors, who come in their hundreds on summer days, giving it a resemblance to Margate beach on a bank holiday, are not always aware of the hazards and tragic accidents have often occurred.

Tilford is best known for its green, a large triangle of turf on which lies a famous cricket pitch where the game has been played for almost one hundred years. The ancient oak on the north side, 10 feet in diameter at its widest point, is reckoned by some to be nine hundred years old and has definitely been there since the middle of the 17th century. The shallow water at the foot of the picturesque bridge is much favoured by canoeists and paddlers in the summer months. The bridge was built by the monks from Waverley Abbey, the first Cistercian monastery in the country, whose ruins stand a mile away.

Stockbridge Pond is the third largest pond in the area. It is said that ice blocks were cut from the pond for the ice house close to Tilford House. Properly used, they kept meat and fish fresh and also served as a cooler to sober up the village drunks. The bobby, rather than walk them three miles into Farnham, shut them in the darkened ice house for the night.

Rushmoor has a road which is known locally as the 'Straight Mile' and leads to the Pride of the Valley inn at Churt.

Churt is the location of Bron-y-de, the home of David Lloyd George when he married his long-time secretary Frances Stevenson in 1943. Here also is an interesting inn, The Crossways, which has altered little over the years. It was known at one stage as The Shant, supposedly on account of the landlady's reply to proposals by her customers.

The Devil's Jumps are three conical hills. On the walk we climb Stony Jump which is owned by the National Trust, the other two being private property. You will have a panoramic view through 360 degrees: to the north-west are the Frensham ponds (although it is only possible to see the Little Pond clearly), to the north is the Hog's Back and the area to the south-east is Hindhead Common and the Devil's Punch Bowl, also in the care of the National Trust. The large outcrop of sandstone gives the hill its name, but how did the Jumps become linked with the Devil? One suggestion is that the Devil, jumping from hill to hill for exercise, was knocked out with a stone thrown by Thor, the god of thunder, whose name is perpetuated in the neighbouring village of Thursley.

Frensham Little Pond is on the other side of Frensham Common to the Great Pond and was formed in 1246. Like its big sister, it too provided fish for the bishops. During the Second World War both Frensham ponds were drained to prevent them from being a directional aid to enemy bombers as they lined up for raids on military targets in the Aldershot area. Local residents can recall retrieving the fish as the water drained away.

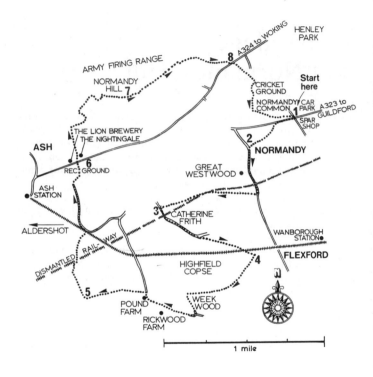

ARMY FIRING RANGE

HENLEY PARK

A324 to WOKING

8

NORMANDY HILL 7

CRICKET GROUND

Start here

NORMANDY COMMON

CAR PARK

1

A323 to GUILDFORD

SPAR SHOP

THE LION BREWERY
THE NIGHTINGALE

ASH

6

REC. GROUND

2

NORMANDY

ASH STATION

GREAT WESTWOOD

ALDERSHOT

DISMANTLED RAILWAY

3

CATHERINE FRITH

WANBOROUGH STATION

4

FLEXFORD

HIGHFIELD COPSE

5

POUND FARM

WEEK WOOD

RICKWOOD FARM

N

1 mile

Ash Village and Normandy Hill

Introduction: Starting from Normandy, this easy, varied walk takes you through fields and woods, skirting the villages of Flexford and Ash, up to the pines of Normandy Hill from where there are lovely views across to the Hog's Back. You then descend through a mass of heather which glows with colour when the flowers are out in late summer.

Distance: The walk is about 6½-miles, circular, and will take around 3 hours.

Refreshments: At Point 6 you have The Nightingale or The Lion Brewery both of which serve bar snacks Monday to Saturday. For hot food on a Sunday there is The Anchor situated half a mile from the car park in the direction of Guildford.

How to get there: The walk commences from the car park opposite the Spar food shop on the A323, which is at a minor crossroads, just past Normandy village, if coming from the direction of Guildford. If coming by train there is an hourly service to Ash station on weekdays, two-hourly on Sundays and you can commence the walk from Point 6. There are several bus routes passing through Ash, where the walk may be commenced at Point 6, and there is an infrequent service to Normandy. (OS maps 186 or SU 85/95 and SU 84/94 [small part only], GR 927516.)

The Walk:
1.   Facing the shop, leave the car park, cross the road and turn right. Immediately after passing a garage turn left over a barrier by a public footpath sign into a field. Walk along past some

15

houses until the end of a fence on the right where you continue diagonally across the field towards a house. Your route may be difficult to locate here but it goes towards a gate which you cross onto an overgrown path leading to a road.

2. Turn left and proceed down the road for about a quarter of a mile, passing Great Westwood on the way. Just the other side of a bridge, cross the road and turn right over a signposted stile. Your route continues with fields on either side and later, after crossing a rather dilapidated stile which is directly beneath power cables, you walk along the edge of another field with woods to your right. Leave the field at the far end to continue direction on a gravelled farm track which takes you through Catherine Frith Woods.

3. At a T-junction turn left and, 30 yards after passing under the power cables, bear right over a stile and then immediately left to maintain direction along the side of a field with the main track parallel on the left. (This path is recommended instead of the main track which can be muddy.) Go over a plank bridge and continue direction along a second field. At the end of this field go through a squeeze stile and immediately bear right over another stile, maintaining direction along the edge of a third field. After passing through an opening in the hedge, bear diagonally right across a field and a drainage ditch towards some dead trees, beyond which is a very tall stile which may be obscured by horse chestnut trees. After going through some woods you climb an embankment and cross the railway line to a stile on the other side leading to an enclosed path bringing you to the outskirts of Flexford (HN).

4. Turn right along a lane past several bungalows. When you reach Beech Tree Farm, turn right onto a track with Highfield Copse on your right and fields on the left. (After wet weather you may find this track extremely muddy and deeply rutted. However, you may find a mud-avoidance path close to the woods on the right.) Continue until your path ends near a fence ahead and turn left on a farm track alongside Week Wood. On reaching a T-junction with a footpath sign, turn right towards the white-painted Rickwood Farmhouse and continue along a tarmaced lane. After passing the barn and well at Pound Farm, turn left on a signposted footpath to pass a pond on your left and the farmhouse on your right. Later you will go under some power cables and, after passing farm buildings on your left, will reach a metalled lane.

5. Turn right at a red-arrowed post onto a very wide, grassy track. This path takes you through some woods and brings you out to a road along which you continue, soon crossing a bridge over a disused railway. Bear right onto a path with a large field on your right and this will lead you to a road where you turn right and shortly go over a railway line. At a road junction turn left and, after about a quarter of a mile, the main road comes into view. Here you should bear right at a footpath sign to cross a recreation field over to the top right corner.

6. Cross the road, with The Nightingale on your right, towards a triangular warning sign, continuing forward under the trees with houses over on your right. Go over a crossing path, then steadily up Normandy Hill, bearing right towards the top of the slope and then keeping a fence on your right. After passing a small gate in the fence, bear left to go over two or three mounds and out to an open area where there will be a small pond on your left (possibly dried out in summer). Ignoring two paths forking right, maintain your north-easterly direction and, on reaching a very large Scots pine in the centre of the path, turn left. Soon you go over a crossing track to reach another track on which you bear right, then right again. This very attractive path continues along the edge of the hill with its dense pinewoods and bears right again, coming to a more open area from which there are good views across to the Hog's Back on the right. Later your path bears round to the left and then forks to the right; you should still be on the edge of the hill. Continue past the first path going steeply downhill. Soon you will reach another and now you are ready for your descent. Before going down, stop to admire the views towards the east from a mound just ahead of you across the path. Continue downhill to the bottom on a very stony track, looking out for a more pleasant path through the heather slightly to the left.

7. Turn left on a wide track and continue for about half a mile, with the Army firing ranges over to your left. Now you join a path coming from your left on which there is a flag-pole. Bear right on this path which becomes very sandy, later ignoring a fork to the right, and follow it until you reach a lane. Turn left down to the main road.

8. Cross the road and go over a short wire fence by another triangular warning sign. This narrow, winding path may be quite overgrown in high summer. It will lead you through the woods of Normandy Common (HN) and eventually emerges onto a cricket ground. Turn right, following round the edge of the field for 100 yards or so and, by some seats, take a small path leading you back into the woods. Continue over a small crossing path and bear left. Ignore small branching paths and, after going over a crossing track, you will reach two cottages which you pass on your right. Continue on a gravelled track to pass a football field on your left. Turn right through a small recreation area towards some tennis courts, passing them on your left, and very shortly you will be back at the car park.

Historical Notes

Normandy is associated with William Cobbett who died there in 1835. The great politician spent his last days at Normandy Farm, but his body was taken back the few miles to Farnham, his birthplace, and buried in the family grave close to the main door of St Andrew's church in the town.

Ash is a parish within the Borough of Guildford but it is always associated with Aldershot because of its close proximity to the Hampshire town. The county boundary is all that separates the two. Old Ash can still be seen between the church of St Peter and the Greyhound public house. A cottage close to the church used to be the Harts Horn Inn where, it is said, Dick Turpin was a visitor. Ribbon development between Ash and Ash Vale has taken away any last vestige of village appearance but Ash Green to the south remains pleasantly rural. Nearby at Wyke some residents are engaged in a battle with oilmen over exploration on their land.

Flexford derives its name from flax-weir, i.e. weir by which flax grows.

Normandy Common was a place where pigs were a problem for users back in the 1920s. They obstructed the footpaths and made them dirty and parish councillors won permission from the War Office to erect stiles and gates to stop animals from leaving the commons, although the paths remained unfenced.

Newlands Corner and Albury Downs

Introduction: This is a moderately energetic walk, with a variety of scenery including farmland and woods and you will be close to the River Tilling Bourne for part of the route. There are superb views from St Martha's Hill and Newlands Corner (HN) which, at 567 feet above sea level, is one of the North Downs' most popular vantage points. There are optional diversions into the villages of Chilworth and Shalford.

Distance: The walk is a 7-mile circuit and will take around $3\frac{1}{4}$–$3\frac{1}{2}$ hours.

Refreshments: There is a hamburger stall in the car park at the start, with a range of food and drink. On the A25 at Newlands Corner is a hotel, The Manor at Newlands, which offers a good range of bar snacks and meals. In addition there are two cafes nearby. About a third of the way along the walk you pass close to the Percy Arms at Chilworth where the menu is varied. If you make the optional visit to Shalford you will find an inn, The Sea Horse, there.

How to get there: The walk commences from Newlands Corner which is on the A25, south-east of Guildford and west of Dorking. The Green Line 773 passes through Newlands Corner and there are several bus services going through Chilworth and Shalford from where the walk may be joined between Points 5 and 6 and Point 8 respectively. There is a large car park and picnic area from where the walk begins. (OS maps 186, or TQ 04/14, GR 044492.)

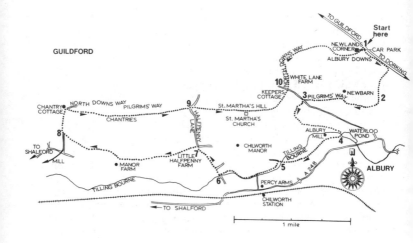

The Walk:

1. From the car park walk back towards the road but, just before reaching it, turn right onto a stony track, crossing the signposted North Downs Way (HN). When the path divides at an old wartime pillbox (HN), take the right fork which leads you to an open area on your right. Here you should bear left, keeping on the main track and later ignoring a farm track off to the right.

2. Immediately after passing a track coming in from the left turn right up to a signposted public bridleway, shortly going through a gateway. There is a clear view of Newbarn Farm on your right. At the end of this path turn right towards the farmhouse and then, very soon, left to maintain direction on a sandy bridleway with woods to the left and fields to the right.

3. On reaching a road, cross this diagonally left to a bridleway which brings you to a small parking area. Turn right and go through a wooden barrier to take the left, grassy, path which descends steeply and eventually bears left. You will come to a particularly attractive spot with views of the Tilling Bourne river down through beech trees to your right. When the path ends go through a barrier, turn right past Millstream Cottage and walk towards a footpath sign ahead with Waterloo Pond on your left.

4. At the footpath sign turn right and pass Albury Mill and trout farm. As the path bears left, you should turn right to take a signposted footpath alongside a private drive. Cross a stile and maintain direction along the side of a field, passing a pond on your right. Go across a plank bridge to another stile, then make your way over a field with a ditch to your left. Having cleared yet another stile, bear slightly to the right across a small field towards a further stile by a signpost.

5. Turn right on a farm track, go over a bridge and then turn left alongside the Tilling Bourne (HN). Just ahead you will see the remains of some old gunpowder factories on the right (HN). Later the path divides. (If refreshments are required, bear left here and go over a footbridge to a hedged track which will bring you alongside a school and out to a road. Turn left for 100 yards to the Percy Arms at Chilworth (HN). Afterwards retrace your steps to the point where you left the route). Keep straight ahead and eventually you will pass some old millstones on your right. Later the track ends at an iron gate by West Lodge.

6. Turn right along a road and at a bend turn left over a drive and up a signposted footpath. (If you wish to view Chilworth Manor (HN), turn right at this point up Halfpenny Lane. You will then need to retrace your steps.) At the top of this path you will reach a road.

7. Turn immediately left through a farm gate. Walk between two fields, with a fence on your left, eventually passing an old barn on your right. Keep to this track, ignoring stiles to the right and left. When you reach Manor Farm you should turn right over a stile but maintain direction along the side of a field with a hedge on your left. Go over a stile and continue in the same direction along the side of the next field with the green spire of Shalford Church straight ahead. Soon you will see Guildford Cathedral (HN) on the horizon diagonally right. Maintain direction on the path, which now runs unfenced between two fields, to reach a stile and a road.

If you wish to visit Shalford (HN) with its mill and church, turn left along this small residential road and immediately left again onto a small footpath running parallel to the road. Cross a road to some steps and a stile opposite, then continue forward through a field, alongside a barbed-wire fence. A bridge now takes you over the Tilling Bourne to the mill. From the mill walk to the main road where you turn right. The Sea Horse is opposite and further down the road you will find the church. To continue the walk retrace your steps to the stile where you left the route.

8. Turn right along the road, soon bearing right onto a sandy footpath. Just before Chantry Cottage, turn right at the sign for Chantry Woods and climb uphill taking the path to the left of a wooden hut. At a junction of paths by a seat maintain direction uphill. At the top you will reach a clearing with seats on both sides of the track and pass a post with a figure 7 on your right. Continue downhill towards a tree with a circular seat where the paths divide and you bear right. Ignore the directions of red posts and keep ahead soon going up some steps. Continue in the same direction when two paths come in from the right and you will reach a road.

9. Turn left along the road for a few yards and then right onto the North Downs Way by the side of Southernway Cottage. Go through wooden bars onto a wide sandy track. At the top of St Martha's Hill you will come to St Martha's Church (HN). After viewing the church maintain your original, easterly direction descending now on a wide, fenced, sandy track. When the track forks, bear left at the North Downs Way sign. At the next fork keep left and, just before reaching a road, turn left and then immediately right at another North Downs Way sign. (This path can be extremely muddy so one can use the road instead which goes in the same direction, passing a stables and White Lane Farm on the right.)

10. At a further North Downs Way sign, turn right and go through wooden bars, keeping right at an acorn sign and eventually coming to the open area of Albury Downs. Bear diagonally left uphill and, on reaching the top, keep on any of the three main paths following the contour of the hill. You pass several turnings to the left and later the three paths merge into one track. After about a quarter of a mile your path bears left uphill between two posts towards the car park.

Historical Notes

Newlands Corner has always been a favourite viewpoint. On a clear day you can see Chanctonbury Ring on the South Downs. At one particular spot a whole range of Surrey hills are visible from Reigate and Leith Hills in the east to Blackdown and

Hindhead in the west. The grove of yew trees which shades the track here is mentioned in the Domesday Book.

The North Downs Way is one of the most ancient arteries of communication in Britain. The first settlers, who arrived 6,000 years ago, followed this high road above the impenetrable forests of the Weald.

Pill Boxes were erected all along the North Downs before the beginning of World War II in anticipation of a threatened German invasion.

The River Tilling Bourne on this stretch is a spot where jewel-weed (orange balsam) grows. It was first found growing wild in England on the river Wey by John Stuart Mill in 1822.

Chilworth, being a good site for a water-wheel, was a centre of industry for centuries. There was a mill listed in the Domesday Book, corn and fulling mills were situated in Chilworth in 1589 and gunpowder was manufactured here as early as 1580. In Queen Anne's reign they manufactured bank notes, too. During Charles I's reign, in 1625, the East India Company set up more extensive mills making gunpowder and cordite but the Chilworth Gunpowder Company was not formed until 1885. Six men were killed in an explosion at the gunpowder works in 1901. 'The most terrible accident which it has ever been our painful duty to record,' said the "Surrey Advertiser". The explosion, soon after the men's breakfast break, blasted the two-storey Black Corning House to pieces.

Chilworth Manor has origins going back to Saxon times and was once owned by Sarah, widow of the great Duke of Marlborough.

Guildford's Cathedral of the Holy Spirit is situated on the top of Stag Hill. It was designed in 1932 by Sir Edward Maufe who won the open competition, though building was interrupted for twelve years by the war and its aftermath and it was not consecrated until 1961. Guildford and Liverpool are the only cathedrals in England to be built on new sites since 1250.

Shalford. The church end of the village is full of old houses and cottages and the stocks and whipping post are preserved outside the churchyard wall. The village had an important fair in medieval times, possibly the model of Vanity Fair in "Pilgrims Progress". It was also once an important landing stage when barges plied the Wey. Gunpowder from the Chilworth mills was brought the short distance to the river bank and transferred for the water-borne trip to London. Now pleasure craft use the river which is navigable as far upstream as Godalming. In 1983 it deservedly basked in the glory of winning a section of the county's Best Kept Village competition.

Shalford Mill, which you will pass on your route if going to the village, is early 18th century. It is open to visitors and well worth a visit. The mill operated until 1914 and most of the machinery is intact. It was given to the National Trust in 1932 and was once the property of Major Arthur Godwin-Austen whose family is remembered on tablets in St Mary's church, a Victorian building on the site of the Domesday church. One of the Godwin-Austens explored and surveyed the north-west Himalayas.

St Martha's Church is on the Pilgrims Way to Canterbury and, it is claimed, dates from Saxon times. The original chapel, in which the pilgrims stopped to worship, was damaged by a gunpowder explosion in 1763 which brought down the tower. It was left derelict for many years but rebuilt in 1850 by the Surrey architect, Henry Woodyer. During the 1914–18 war it was covered with a camouflage of fir saplings to prevent it serving as a landmark to the German Zeppelins seeking the powder mills. The earliest documentary evidence of the name is around 1200 and in 1463 Bishop Waynflete of Winchester wrote of 'the chapel dedicated to Sainte Martha the Virgin and all the Holy Martyrs, commonly called Martirhill founded and situated next to the town of Guldeford in our diocese.' There is, according to the chaplain in a letter to the *Surrey Advertiser* in early 1984, a strong tradition that early Christians were martyred there by pagan Saxons about 600 AD as part of the resistance movement to the spread of Christianity. If this were true, he wrote, then Martha could be a corruption of Martyr. 'Those of us connected with the church believe that the dedication of St Martha originated in Norman times and was a deliberate choice,' he added.

R.H.S. Gardens, Wisley and Ockham

Introduction: This easy walk takes you over Ockham and Wisley commons, through pinewoods and farmland, across the disused Wisley Airfield and passes through the villages of Ockham and Martyrs Green. You can combine this walk with a visit to Wisley Royal Horticultural Society Gardens, as at the beginning of the route you will be going through a small section of the grounds, then along the river Wey and past Ockham Mill.

Distance: The walk is an 8-mile circuit and will take around 3½–4 hours.

Refreshments: An obvious and convenient place for a stop, less than halfway through the walk, is The Hautboy in Ockham which has recently been refurbished. A better stop for those in walking gear might be The Black Swan, which serves a good range of hot and cold light meals. If you wish to go to this pub make a slight de-tour when you reach the road leading to Martyrs Green at Point 6. (You could also make a diversion to this inn at Point 7.) There are some fine historical inns at Ripley, particularly The Anchor and The Talbot. The refreshment facilities at the RHS Gardens at Wisley can be used by members, otherwise you can pay admission to the Gardens and explore their delights as well as use the cafe-teria.

How to get there: The walk commences from the car park outside the R.H.S. Gardens near the village of Wisley. Turn off the A3 on the road leading to the Gardens and shortly take a left-hand fork. Go almost to the end of the car park near the exit for Wisley village. There is a good train service to Effingham Junc-tion from where one could easily commence the walk at Point 6.

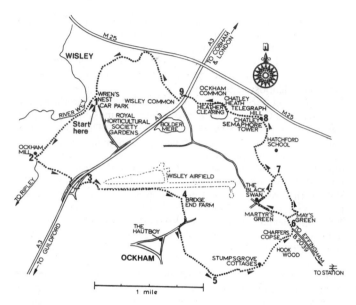

The Green Line 715 passes along the A3 close to Wisley Gardens and there are other routes to Ripley and Ockham from where the walk may be joined at either Point 2 or 3 and between Points 4 and 5 respectively. (OS maps 187 or TQ 05/15, GR 065586.)

The Walk:
1. Leaving the car park at the top turn immediately left over a stile onto a signposted, fenced footpath by Wren's Cottage which takes you past the pinetum area of Wisley Gardens (HN). Soon the river Wey comes into view on your right. At the end of the Gardens continue on a grassy path across a field. Go over a stile and a plank bridge to cross a larger field, keeping to the same direction and later joining a fenced path in the same field. After crossing another stile you will pass some bungalows on your right and come out to a lane.
2. Turn right to view Ockham Mill (HN). (Opposite is a beautiful stretch of water – Mill Tail – which runs into the river Wey.) Retrace your steps and continue forward along the lane to

the road ahead. (100 yards or so on your right there is an optional diversion on a bridleway into Ripley (HN).) The roar of the traffic on the new elevated section of the A3 trunkway will soon be heard. Cross the road to go under the bridge beneath the A3, then cross the road again, turning left past a bus stop towards a signposted footpath.

3. Turn right here to a stile by a metal gate with another public footpath sign. Cross the stile into a field and make for a footpath sign at the top of the ridge on the skyline. (The path may be indistinct as this area has only recently been given public access.) Follow the direction of the sign which leads you across a gravelled area to another stile by a yellow waymark. After crossing this you will be on the runway of the disused Wisley Airfield (HN). Follow the broken yellow lines which zigzag across the runway taking you through two sets of metal barriers at footpath signs. After passing the second set of barriers the lines will lead you into a field. Continue in the same direction towards the buildings of Bridge End Farm.

4. Cross a stile, turn right on a track through the farm, go through a gate and then continue down a lane. At the bottom turn right along a road, where you will pass some very attractive houses, until you reach Beech Cottage. (If you wish to visit Ockham (HN) and The Hautboy at this point continue down the road for another 200 yards or so.) Cross over to a public footpath opposite and then go over a stile to walk along the left edge of a field. This path will take you through a metal barrier to another field, still with the hedge and a ditch on your left, to a stile by some farm buildings and then to a farm track on which you turn left. When you have crossed over a stream bear right towards a stile into a field and cross it diagonally to an opening in the trees at the far corner. Continue in the same diagonal direction across the next field to a stile in the fence near its corner.

5. Enter the woods and continue on a well-defined path, which later widens, until you emerge onto a farm track by a gate. Turn right and soon turn left at the end of a fence. Continue again through the woods until you reach a crossing track just past a sign saying 'SCC Footpath Only – No Horses'. Turn left and shortly you come to a gate by a wooden bridge. Cross a meadow to another gate, by a bridleway sign, which leads you onto a concrete drive past Stumpsgrove Cottage. When the drive bears left continue ahead along the edge of a field to reach Hook

27

Wood. Your route now zigzags through the trees but follows the course of a sunken path (or wide ditch). Ignore all turnings left and right, later going over a wide grassy ride and on towards a brick bridge over which you turn left up to a road.

6. Turn left on the road until it bends to the left. (If you wish to visit The Black Swan continue up the road for about a quarter of a mile to a crossroads. Turn right for another quarter of a mile to resume the walk at Point 7.) To continue the walk, turn right on a lane to May's Green. Just before a junction in the lane turn left over a stile, cross a garden lawn and go through a waymarked gate onto a very brambly, fenced path. Go over a stile and across a field towards a gate to the left of a house ahead. This leads you onto a concreted farm track that later becomes gravelled and you continue ahead with good views over to your right. When this track bears left continue forward on a fenced path to a kissing gate and down some steps to a road. Turn left past Flower Cottage. (You may also leave the walk at this point to continue up the road for a quarter of a mile to The Black Swan.)

7. To continue the walk turn right on a gravelled bridleway leading to Hatchford End and over to your right, nestling in the trees, is Hatchford School (HN). After passing a cottage on the left the track bears left but you turn right at a bridleway sign. About 50 yards further on you will reach a crossing track where you turn left for almost 100 yards. Just before a wooden post you turn right through rhododendron bushes on an uphill path which is usually muddy. (Look for some fine specimens of redwood, some of which are actually on the path.) At a T-junction turn left and on coming to another T-junction turn left again for about 50 yards where you turn right, passing a barrier, towards the Chatley Heath Semaphore Tower (HN).

8. Passing the tower on your right turn left on a wide track marked with a green arrow on a short post. Follow this path downhill and, when the main track bears right, continue forward on a smaller path marked with another green arrow sign. Later you rejoin the main track coming in from the right and continue downhill to a wide crossing track by an open area where you turn right. Follow the sandy path in a semi-circle passing some picnic seats and a track going off to the right. The path now becomes very wide at a junction of several tracks. After passing the last picnic seat ignore two wide tracks on your right, soon turning right into the woods at a green arrowed post. At a fork by two green arrowed posts continue right across a mound and on towards a bridge over the A3.

9. After crossing the bridge make for a car park ahead turning left on a metalled track, then soon turning right on a farm track. Continue forward and ignore a track forking left by a wooden barrier. Later you will pass a large pond on your right and Pond Farmhouse on your left. When the main track forks right towards the M25 continue forward under the trees passing some wooden huts on your left. As you reach the barrier for the M25 turn left and soon your path turns left again, away from the road, at a Surrey County Council 'Open Space' sign. At the end of a field on your right turn right. Almost immediately ignore a left fork and continue on keeping close to the field and the motorway over to your right. After crossing a planked bridge you fork left and later your path is joined by another coming in from the right. Continue forward ignoring several branching paths and soon you will reach the road on which you turn left for the car park.

Historical Notes

Wisley Common was the site of an uproar in 1869 when the locals came to hear of a proposal to enclose 362 of its acres, and the plan was dropped. Since then, development has eroded much of the countryside but Bolder Mere remains. It is a 10-acre shallow lake, currently favoured by wind-surfers and previously beloved of customers of the Hut Hotel which once stood just across the Portsmouth Road. Sadly, that hostelry was demolished in the name of progress when this stretch of the A3 was transformed into a dual carriageway in 1976. Early in the last century this common, and others nearby, yielded deposits of Epsom salt.

Wisley village is a little less than a mile from the starting point and very rural. The lane which serves as the main street wanders between houses, crosses quite a wide stretch of the Wey and bends past the little Norman church, restored in 1872. Beside the church, which has no dedication, is a delightful 17th-century farmhouse that was once the vicarage.

29

Wisley Royal Horticultural Society Gardens are, of course, the village's main claim to fame. Besides the thousands of visitors who walk round the lovely acres every year, millions more are familiar with the place through the Gardener's Calendar programme on Channel 4. The gardens came into the possession of the R.H.S. following the death of the society's treasurer. Mr G. F. Wilson, who owned 60 acres of shrubs and flowers at Wisley.

Ockham Mill is dated 1862 but the present building is a mixture of various additions made since. The half-timbered mill house opposite has one of the loveliest gardens in the whole of Surrey.

Ripley has been a popular venue for cricketers and cyclists since the last century. Cricket was played on the Green near the main road and cycling was centred around the gabled and low-ceilinged Anchor Inn. Cricket is still played in the village and cyclists continue to call.

Wisley Airfield had an important role to play during World War II but it does not have the repute of the more famous Battle of Britain airfields. After the war it was used by the Vickers aircraft manufacturing company, based nearby on the old Brooklands car racing track near Weybridge, for some of its experimental work. When it was no longer required for this purpose it remained fenced off to the public, even though public rights of way had existed over it before the war. In the early 80's there were plans afoot to turn it into a private executive jet airfield but the public outcry that ensued put paid to this project and, after much campaigning, the area was reopened for public use in 1985.

Ockham, which nestles quietly to the east of the new A3, and even newer M25, has long been dominated by its park which was bought by the first Lord King who was Queen Anne's Lord Chancellor. It eventually passed into the hands of his descendants, the Lovelaces, whose name is used to indicate the local ward on the Guildford Borough Council. In the park stands All Saint's Church much of which is 13th-century, including the seven-light east window, possibly brought from Newark Priory at the dissolution of Monasteries. The nave has a wagon roof above tie-beams, circa 1530.

Hatchford House became Hatchford Park School, a preparatory school for boys, in the early part of the century.

Chatley Heath Semaphore Tower is an impressive monument to the days when telegraphs connected London, through Surrey, to the sea. During the Napoleonic Wars and in the early 19th century it was a vital link in a chain of hilltop stations which sent messages to and from the Admiralty in London to the nation's main naval base at Portsmouth. It was restored to its former glory during 1986.

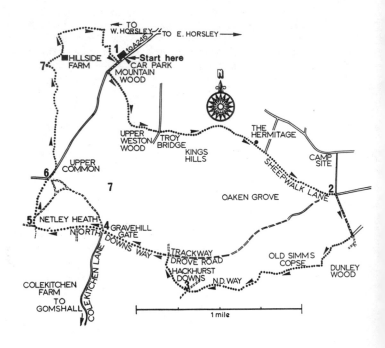

The North Downs Way and Mountain Wood

Introduction: Here is a good ramble for all times of the year which is also fairly easy. It almost manages to avoid going through any areas of human habitation and, in fact, only passes five or six houses on the whole route. There are, nonetheless, some interesting places to visit before or afterwards and you have directions for an optional diversion into Gomshall. As a walk for a hot summer day, or when rain threatens, it has the advantage for being under trees for most of the time.

Distance: Around 2¾–3 hours is needed for this 7-mile circuit. The distance may be reduced by half a mile towards the end but this would require walking along a fairly busy road for about three-quarters of a mile. An optional diversion into Gomshall (HN) will add approximately two miles to the walk.

Refreshments: There are some good places to eat and drink close to the route. Leaving the car park, you can turn right towards Shere where there are one or two good choices. Otherwise, turn left to East Horsley and visit the Duke of Wellington which serves excellent ale and where you can obtain a hearty meal at a reasonable price. If walking on a Sunday, it might be advisable to book a table in advance. In Gomshall there is the White Horse Inn which always has a good selection of hot and cold food.

How to get there: To reach the car park for Mountain Wood, from where the walk commences, leave the A246 half a mile east of East Horsley on the road signposted to Green Dene and Sheep Leas. Continue down the road for almost one and a half miles and you will find the small Green Dene car park on your right. It is possible to join the walk at point 4 if you are coming by train. There is an hourly service to Gomshall on weekdays and two-hourly on Sundays. Buses run to East Horsley, which is about a mile away from the starting point. Better served is Gomshall which is about a mile from point 4. (OS maps 187 or TQ 05/15 & TQ 04/14, GR 091509.)

The Walk:

1. From the car park turn right along the road for about 200 yards, then left onto a signposted bridleway where you pass a water tank and climb up into Mountain Wood. At the end of a flat area of deforestation on your right keep left with the main track. This rough path now descends steeply to a forestry road which you cross, continuing ahead. (It can be extremely muddy here so, if necessary, look for a mud-avoidance path to the right for part of the way.) You should ignore a right fork and, after going under Troy Bridge and then another Lovelace (HN) bridge you will pass a house (The Hermitage) on the left. Soon you will come out onto a drive, passing another house on the right. Go through a forestry gate and at a junction of paths continue on the main, left-bearing track, soon passing a disused army camp. Eventually you will come to a T-junction.

2. Turn left onto a very wide track and, after about 100 yards, turn right onto a sandy track with a wire fence on the right and a series of tree stumps on the left. After a quarter of a mile, on reaching a wooden post, turn right on a well-defined path into Dunley Wood. Your path winds through the wood and eventually bears right to join another track coming in from the left. You soon pass a green wooden post as you continue through Old Simm's Copse. On reaching a T-junction turn left to reach the end of the wood, soon passing a turning on the right. Almost immediately turn right over a stile onto Blatchford Down (HN) and the North Downs Way. At the end of an open area, where there are fine views to the left, cross another stile by a gate into woods. Your path eventually joins a main track coming in from the right and soon you will come to the open area of Hackhurst Downs (HN). (You may wish to stop here as this is a good point at which to take a rest and admire the view of Gomshall and beyond towards the south-west. Bee and fly orchids are found in this area but if you are fortunate enough to find some, please leave them for others to enjoy.)

3. Just before the path starts to descend steeply you bear right onto a path with a wire fence on the left. Ignore a stile on your left and continue until you reach the main trackway where you should turn left at a North Downs Way signpost opposite a disused water tank. Keep to the main track for about three-quarters of a mile, ignoring all side turnings.

4. On reaching another disused water tank, at Gravehill Gate, there is a junction of paths. (If you wish to take the diversion into Gomshall, turn left at this point and continue downhill, soon passing Colekitchen Farm, to the steep embankments of Cole-kitchen Lane. On reaching the main road, the A25, you are in Gomshall. After your visit retrace your steps up Colekitchen Lane to the water tank, where you should turn left.) Continue forward and when the track bears left, go straight ahead on a grassy path, with Netley Heath over on your right. Later you rejoin the main track and after about 100 yards, just beyond a track turning to the left, you will see a path on the right.

5. Turn right downhill through the trees and out to a tarmac drive which you should cross to the path opposite. Keep to it for about a quarter of a mile and you will come out to a road.

6. Turn right along the road and soon left on a signposted bridleway, keeping right where the path forks. Later your path leaves the woods and you continue direction between fields. Another bridleway comes in from the right and you continue down towards a lane on which you turn right. The lane later curves left uphill past some bungalows on the left and soon you will see some large black tanks on your right.

7. Turn right on a track leading down to some farm buildings. Your route continues through the farm and you will have fine views over to your left. At a T-junction turn left and continue on a concreted drive. As the field on your right ends turn right on a fenced, tree-lined path. You will enter some woods at a public bridleway sign and then you should immediately turn right by two tree stumps. On reaching an arrowed post turn right and after about 200 yards turn left into woods. On reaching a T-junction turn right on a little path which will lead you down to the car park.

Historical Notes

Gomshall is well-known for its beauty, its 16th century pack-horse bridge and watercress beds. A tannery, dating back at least to the 11th century, has a shop where you may possibly find some bargains in leather goods.

Horsleys – The twin Horsley villages – East and West – with their pleasant rural features are both worth visiting. In East Horsley you will find Horsley Towers which is quite an unusual building for this part of the country. The present Towers, which has been a training establishment for some years, dates from the mid-1800s when most of East Horsley was rebuilt under the direction of the Earl of Lovelace. St Martin's Church, which is nearby, is also well worth a visit.

The Earl of Lovelace is closely associated with this area, which is in the Parish of East Horsley, and his influence is particularly apparent in many of the old houses with their distinctive flint walls. During the walk you pass under two Lovelace bridges: Troy and Hermitage. They cross a track, running eastwards from the south end of Honeysuckle Bottom, which was a road in the last century and is still named Sheepwalk Lane. Dotted all over the woods in the area, the curious horseshoe-shaped bridges usually span gulleys or deep lanes. Lord Lovelace and his woodsmen used them to transport timber from place to place. Whatever other considerations presented themselves, durability of structure was not one of them. Many are barely traceable and some have disappeared altogether.

Hackhurst Downs, whose name derives from the Anglo-Saxon heah-hyrst meaning high wood, has marvellous views. Sheep grazing has been reintroduced into the area in an attempt to return it to its former glory. The droveway, which forms part of the North Downs Way, is a very ancient track but was tarmaced during World War II for the Canadian forces who also used the army camp, the remains of which you pass on the walk.

Blatchford Down was named in the memory of Alan Blatchford who died suddenly in 1980. Alan was a keen Surrey walker who was particularly fond of this part of the North Downs. He was a founder member of the Long Distance Walkers' Association and was for some time its National Secretary. It was he who initially organised Britain's first walkers' marathon, the "Tanners". His widow, Barbara, is Senior Principal Rights of Way Officer for Surrey County Council and is also very much involved with the LDWA.

Holmbury St Mary and Ewhurst

Introduction: This moderate walk will reward you with fine views from Holmbury and Pitch Hills and passes the peaceful villages of Ewhurst and Peaslake. The vicinity is rich in evidence of Roman occupation and you will be following little-used paths in an otherwise well-trodden area. At Point 2 there is a steep, downhill path requiring care, especially in wet conditions.

Distance: The walk is a 7-mile circuit and will take around 3–3½ hours.

Refreshments: During the walk you could stop at The Bulls Head at Ewhurst or The Hurtwood Inn at Peaslake, both of which offer bar snacks. A short detour before climbing Pitch Hill will take you to The Windmill which always has a good selection of hot food. At Holmbury St Mary there is the choice of either The Royal Oak or The Kings Head. On the way back to the A25, you will find The Volunteer, at Sutton Abinger and this is a popular pub with walkers.

How to get there: The walk commences from the parking area opposite the Youth Hostel near Holmbury St Mary. Turn off the A25 onto the B2126 and go through Sutton Abinger (HN). Just before the village of Holmbury St Mary (HN) turn right up a lane signposted for Radnor Lane, Woodhouse Lane and the youth hostel. Continue to the end where you will find a small, open area by Hurtwood Common. There are infrequent bus services to Holmbury St Mary, which is about half a mile from the start of the walk, and to Ewhurst from where the walk may be joined at Point 3. (OS maps 187 or TQ 04/14, GR 104451.)

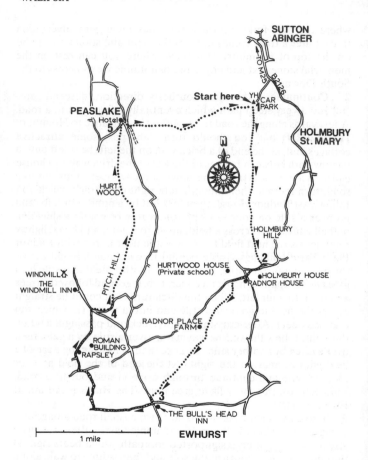

The Walk:

1. With your back to the youth hostel, leave the parking area on a path straight ahead, passing a "Hurtwood Control" notice on your left. You will come to a wide, heather-lined, sandy track where you turn left to go steadily uphill, eventually crossing a wide track. Continue for another quarter of a mile, going over a small crossing track and ignoring a turning left, then bear left on a wide, grassy path. After passing two crossing tracks bear left

38

where the path forks onto a sandy track lined with silver birch trees. Later a track comes in from the right and soon you will be on the top of Holmbury Hill (HN) where you can rest on the memorial stone seat and enjoy the panoramic views across to the South Downs.

2. Continuing in the same southerly direction, descend carefully on a very steep path which eventually brings you to a road. A few yards along the road to the left is the entrance to Holmbury House (HN) but you should turn right past some attractive cottages and, at the end of a brick wall on the left, bear left onto a narrow path between hedges to the left of the driveway to a house called Wayfarers. After going down some wooden steps out to a road, turn left and then immediately right on a track which you follow past Radnor House, then fork left by a pond. Look for and go over a stile on your left opposite a row of conifers shielding netball courts. Go across a field, down to a gate, and bear slightly right across the next field to cross a stile near a tree with Radnor Place Farm buildings visible behind it. Continue straight across the field to a further stile, then across another field to a stile by a gate and footpath sign, over a concrete bridge, and follow the trees and ditch to your left. When the ditch turns left continue straight across the field to go over a stile and into a wood (in which you may see deer). After crossing a farm track and passing a field on the right, follow the yellow waymarks over a stile by a gate, then over a ditch by another stile. Your path then follows the edge of a field with railings on the right. At the end of the field go over another stile and continue through a wood and out to a road. Turn left towards the village green and The Bull's Head inn at Ewhurst (HN).

3. Cross the village green and go down a small road alongside a garage. After about half a mile and immediately after crossing a stream, turn right on a signposted footpath which bears right at the end of a field. Cross a metal stile and then a ditch to walk along the left side of a field, go through a gate, turn left down the road, and almost immediately turn right on a drive leading to Rapsley. When the metalled track ends at Rapsley Cottage (HN) on your right keep ahead on the bridleway through the trees. Ignore a turning on your right and continue ahead going steadily uphill. Immediately after passing some houses on the right, turn right through short metal posts to reach a road. (Turn left along the road for a quarter of a mile if you wish to visit The Windmill inn.) Cross to the road opposite and follow this past some houses on the right.

4. On reaching a fork, take the left-hand, rough track going steadily up to the ridge of Pitch Hill (HN), where there are fine views. Continue along this broad sandy track, ignoring all turnings, for about a mile and a half. (Hurt Wood is over to your left and, eventually, on the horizon on a clear day you will see St Martha's Church on St Martha's Hill near Guildford). At the end of this fine ridge path you will reach a cemetery on your left and, at a junction of paths, take the one to the right which leads you past a church and into the village of Peaslake (HN) opposite the "Hurtwood Inn".

5. Turn right up the road and, just after the village cross, turn left up Radnor Road for a few yards and then almost immediately turn left again up a steep path opposite a private garage. At the top cross over onto a hedged path, which takes you to a wooded area where you continue forward downhill. Go over two crossing tracks, continue uphill past a wooden post and, after some way, on coming to a fork, keep to your left. Go through an opening in a fence and continue in the same direction over several crossing tracks. Your route continues on a path through the woods which dips and rises and is sunken in parts. At a point where the path curves round to the right and becomes a wide, well-defined track, you should leave it to continue straight ahead. In a short while you will be back at the parking place by the YHA hostel.

Historical Notes

Sutton Abinger has two old farm houses. Sutton Place Farm was built around 1700. Fulvens is earlier and reputed to be one of the best farms in the county.

Holmbury St Mary, which takes its name from St Mary's Church, built in 1879, is not hard to imagine as it was a century or more ago. The area was one of the wildest in Surrey, and sheep stealers, smugglers and poachers took refuge in the remote hills. Many of the cottages had large cellars where contraband was hidden.

Holmbury Hill is 857 ft above sea level which leaves it short of

Hindhead and Leith Hill. It is the site of an 8-acre Iron Age settlement dating from 150 BC. The earthworks of double banks and ditches, which once had a stockade between them, can still be seen surrounding all but the steep south-facing slope. In Guildford Museum there is a collection of artefacts, including many flint tools and pottery shards, which were found when the site was excavated in the 1930s.

Holmbury House, built in the 1860s, was once owned by the Guinness family and later became a school. Today, the sign outside proclaims it to be the Mullard Space Science Laboratory. It is part of University College, London, and was set up in 1965 following a generous gesture by the Mullard Company. It stemmed from a space research group set up in the 1950s in the college, which had already established a worldwide reputation.

Ewhurst has an old but much restored church, St Peter and St Paul, which is a short way down the road from the green. 'Tinkering repairs' to the ancient central part of the tower and its wooden steeple in 1839 brought the lot crashing down and it was mostly rebuilt. The windmill at Ewhurst was, at 800 ft above sea level, a notable landmark but work ceased in 1885 and it was converted into a house around the turn of the century.

Rapsley is the site of a Roman courtyard villa which was discovered in 1956. It had a bathhouse on the east side, an aisled hall to the west and, on the south side, a timbered building with an apsidal end which may have been a shrine. Its date of occupancy has been put at 35–80 AD and the inhabitants probably made tiles and raised cattle. The villa was unearthed when Hareholt Copse was being replanted; archaeologists completed the work in 1968.

Pitch Hill is also a site of Roman activity, especially in the second century. There are many properties in the surrounding area built of Pitch Hill stone.

Peaslake is one of Surrey's most secluded villages, tucked away on the slopes of Hurt Wood which was given to the public for 'air and exercise' in the 1920s. The Bray family of Shere, in whose parish Peaslake is situated. has quarried the local hillside for generations.

41

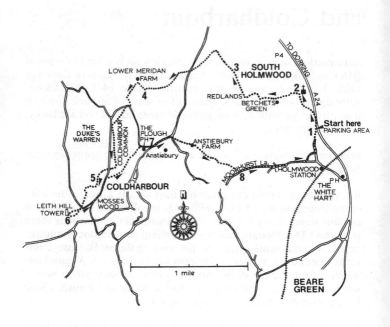

LOWER MERIDAN
FARM

SOUTH
HOLMWOOD

P4

TO DORKING

3

REDLANDS

BETCHETS
GREEN

2

A24

4

Start here
PARKING AREA

1

THE
DUKE'S
WARREN

COLDHARBOUR
COMMON

THE
PLOUGH
PH 7

ANSTIEBURY
FARM

Anstiebury

MOORHURST La.

8

HOLMWOOD
STATION

5

COLDHARBOUR

PH
THE
WHITE
HART

LEITH HILL
TOWER

6

MOSSES
WOOD

N

BEARE
GREEN

1 mile

Leith Hill
and Coldharbour

Introduction: This moderately energetic walk is from Holmwood (HN) and takes you through Redlands onto the eastern slopes of Leith Hill and through the historic village of Coldharbour. Although it may have more than its fair share of ups and downs it is an attractive walk with magnificent views and, if you are lucky, you may see deer.

Distance: The walk is a 7-mile circuit and will take approximately 3–3½ hours.

Refreshments: These are available from a little kiosk in the base of the tower on top of Leith Hill. It is usually open on weekends and fine days during the year. In the village of Coldharbour there is an inn, The Plough, and a shop selling confectionery and ice cream. Conveniently close to the end of the walk, just a few yards beyond the station in Holmwood, there is The White Hart which offers a range of hot and cold food. A short drive northwards up the A24 will bring you to the Holly and Laurel which has an excellent range of well-cooked food.

How to get there: Leave the A24 between Dorking and Beare Green where you see a signpost to Holmwood Station. The walk commences from an access road immediately on the right after leaving the main road. Try to avoid parking in front of the cottages. On weekdays there is an infrequent service to Holmwood Station but there are no trains on Sundays. There are bus services along the A24, from where the walk commences, and a very infrequent one from Dorking to Coldharbour where the walk may be joined at Point 7. (OS maps 187 or TQ 04/14, GR 174438.)

The Walk:
1. Leave the access road and continue along the A24 in the direction of Dorking. After passing the drive to Vigo Farm and a bus stop the pavement ends and here you bear left onto a gravelled track. Go past the Holmwood Scout & Guide Centre, then through a barrier and across a green to join an enclosed path leading to South Holmwood church (HN).
2. Opposite the church gate turn left on a path going downhill, ignoring another path branching right. On reaching a lane turn left over a bridge soon passing Betchets Green Farm. At a fork continue right on a drive through brick gate posts until you reach a house called The Lodge where you turn right on a signposted footpath towards another house. Just before the house turn left over a stile continuing along the edge of a field and over two more stiles in quick succession. Having entered a wood turn right onto a path going in a north-westerly direction through conifers, passing a field on your right and then bearing away left uphill. Later there will be another field on your right and you will reach a crossing track.
3. Turn right to continue on a wide, sandy forest road. At the top of a slope your track bears left to a junction of paths and you continue on the sandy road past a water tank on your right. Later another track comes in from the right and 50 yards further on you turn right off the main sandy track onto a grassy one through the trees which will lead you to a gate and out to a road. Turn left on the road for just a few yards to a small parking area. Here you turn sharp right, go through some short posts, then continue forward through woods to a gate and a crossing track. Now bear slightly left to take the middle of three paths going downhill into a valley. Your path goes across a ditch and then rises up to a crossing track.
4. Turn right on this well-defined track and follow it to the entrance to Lower Meridan Farm where you turn left uphill. Cross a wide forestry road and proceed uphill to the next wide track where you turn left. After about 250 yards you will see a static water tank at which you turn right onto a sunken track, immediately ignoring another track turning right and shortly going past a sign for Coldharbour Common. When the path divides at a 'No Horses' sign painted on a tree keep right and, on reaching a hollow at a junction of several paths, bear round to your right through a gap in some beech trees. Continue ahead on

a rising path past a thick wooden post and a waymarked post on your left. In a short while you will come to a crossing track.

5. Turn left and continue along over a crossing track marked by a post with a red band. At another crossing track continue direction along the edge of the hill. Leave this main track where it goes steeply uphill and branch right. Still following the red posts, turn right at a crossing track. After passing a sign for Duke's Warren on your left continue ahead on a narrow path keeping to the edge of Cockshot Hollow, a deep gully, and soon you will be at Leith Hill Tower (HN).

6. From the tower return downhill, this time descending on a wider track and, when you reach Cockshot Hollow again, turn right on a crossing track. Shortly the path divides and you keep to your right. On reaching a signpost for Mosses Wood bear to your left. You will now be walking along the edge of the hill and enjoying fine views to your right. Later your path swings away and you continue to your left, passing another red post, then going under some fine beech trees. At a crossing track ignore the direction of the red post and continue ahead, later going over another crossing track. It will not be long before you see a cricket ground over to your left. Bear right onto a wide track coming from the left and this will lead you all the way down to the village of Coldharbour (HN).

7. On reaching the road at The Plough inn turn left and proceed along the road for a quarter of a mile to a junction where you turn right. Soon turn left on the concreted drive of Anstiebury Farm (HN). After passing through the farm buildings and a gate, you then turn right over a stile and head diagonally right across a field towards the far right-hand corner where you cross another stile. Go downhill through some woods, with a wire fence on your left, to a further stile and then out into a field. You should cross the field to an opening in the right-hand corner. Now keep to the hedge on the left and you will come to a bar stile and out into Moorhurst Lane.

8. Turn left and, after passing a lake, continue along for another half a mile. Later the lane curves left and brings you out to a road where you turn left and will soon be back at the starting point. (If you wish to go to the station, continue forward when the lane curves left past a kissing gate and onto an enclosed path. This leads to another kissing gate and the road on which turn right.)

Historical Notes

Holmwood is close to Holmwood Common which was once the haunt of highwaymen and smugglers. It is now owned by the National Trust, thanks to a gift by the Duke of Norfolk in 1956. Until the 18th century the largest stags in England were hunted at Holmwood. Wild boar, too, were pursued to the death. Wild strawberries were plentiful and taken to market by the cartload.

St Mary Magdalene Church, at South Holmwood, was built in 1838 and the site for it, a parsonage and a school, were given by the Duke of Norfolk.

Leith Hill is 965 feet above sea level, the highest point in the south-east of England. A height of 1000 feet can be attained by climbing to the top of the tower which was originally built in 1766 by Richard Hull of Leith Hill Place. He died in 1772 and by his wish was buried in the tower. Around 1778 it was used by smugglers to signal to the south coast but it fell into decay and was restored in 1795 and the lower part filled with rubble. At some later period a turret was added giving access to the roof. It is said that thirteen counties may be seen from the top on a clear day and two landmarks to look for are the Post Office Tower and St Pauls in central London. On a very clear day it is claimed that the sea, some thirty miles away, has been glimpsed.

When the refreshment hut on the top of the hill fell into disrepair the amenity was moved to the base of the tower. Until recently this was run by Louise Weller who retired at the age of 80. When she arrived in 1933 the water (carried by her father on a yoke) was boiled on an open fire and Louise often slept under a tree ready to brew up at sunrise.

Coldharbour, at almost 800 ft, is one of the highest villages in Surrey. The King's High Way, the old London to Arundel road, passes through. The village is still known as 'The Harbour', i.e. a resting place on a journey. In the 17th century criminals from the assizes at Dorking were hanged on Gallows Hill. The cricket pitch, which you pass on the walk, is the highest in Surrey.

Anstiebury Farm is close to a site where there is much evidence of occupation during the Iron Age and Roman periods. It was used during the Napoleonic wars to shelter women and children from Dorking while the men fought the French.

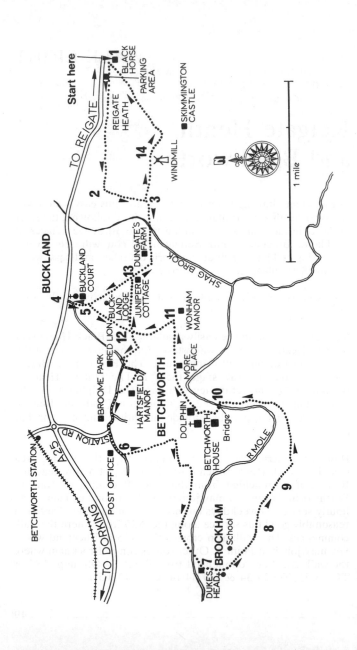

Reigate Heath and Betchworth

Introduction: Starting from Reigate Heath, this easy walk takes you over heath and farmland, here and there following the river Mole. It includes an area bounded by the attractive villages of Buckland, Brockham and Betchworth. You will see several interesting buildings, including historic churches, and pass two of the loveliest village greens in Surrey.

Distance: An 8-mile circuit, it will take approximately 3½–4 hours.

Refreshments: These are easily available. The Black Horse is at Reigate Heath where the walk starts. On the outward leg of the walk a short detour will bring you to The Red Lion at Betchworth. At the halfway stage there is The Duke's Head in Brockham. On the return leg you pass The Dolphin at Betchworth. Finally, there is The Skimmington Castle on Reigate Heath. All of these pubs provide lunchtime and evening bar meals.

How to get there: The walk commences from the parking area near The Black Horse which is off the A25 just before reaching Reigate if approaching from the west. If coming by train to Betchworth station you may join the walk at Point 6. There is an hourly service on weekdays but no trains on Sundays. There is a reasonably good bus service along the A25 from where the walk commences. The walk also crosses the A25 in Buckland where you may join it at Point 4. Other routes run to Brockham where the walk could be commenced from Point 7. (OS maps 187 or TQ 25/35, TQ 24/34 & TQ 04/14, GR 243505.)

The Walk:

1. From The Black Horse by Reigate Heath (HN) head across playing fields towards a sports pavilion, passing it on your left and continuing on a path through conifers. When you reach an open area with seats, turn right onto a wide track, following it until you come to a pine-covered mound. Here you turn left on a path leading past a further mound. Now the path divides and you take the far right fork through a gully and down towards a lane. Turn right and, very soon, left onto a footpath. Continue over a crossing track and, just before reaching the main road, turn left over a stile onto an enclosed footpath with a field on your left. Cross the next stile into a field, following the hedge on your right, but when the hedge bears right go straight ahead towards a gate and public footpath sign.

2. At the sign turn left to follow the edge of a field with a wire fence on your right. Keep to the fence and when you reach a stile continue on a path, with the wire fence now on your left, until you come to the next stile.

3. Turn right into a lane and bear right at a gate with Shag Brook on your right. Shortly you will be passing through Dungate's Farm. When you come to Juniper Cottage on your left, proceed along Dungate's Lane for a quarter of a mile or so, passing sandpit workings on the right, Buckland Lodge on the left and then the high wall of Buckland Court on the right. At the end of the lane you will reach the village store on the main A25 road. (Bear right for a few yards if you wish to visit Buckland church.) Cross the road to the village green (HN).

4. Retrace your steps down Dungate's Lane as far as Buckland Lodge.

5. Bear right, with Buckland Lodge on your left, onto a bridleway leading to a gate. Here you turn right over a stile and into a field. Head for two small huts near some conifers, go over a stile onto a footpath and then turn right. You will reach a house on your left where you go down some steps leading to a road where you turn left to Sandy Lane. (If refreshments are required you should continue down the road for a short distance to The Red Lion and afterwards return to Sandy Lane on which you turn right.) Turn left up Sandy Lane and after passing two houses, turn right through a gate by Hartsfield Lodge with stables on your right. Go through a kissing gate and bear slightly right up a field towards another kissing gate. Cross a drive to a third kissing

gate into a field. There are fine views of Boxhill and the Betch-worth Clump ahead and the large house away on your left is Harts-field Manor. Go down the slope, over a bar stile and on to a kissing gate to the left of some pines. Once you have passed a house and garden, bear left to a footpath taking you down to a road. Turn left and later ignore a turning on the left, then continue past Broome Park and Station Road on the right. You will eventually come to Betchworth Village Store and Post Office on the right, opposite which there is a signposted footpath. Disregard this and look for a signposted bridleway a few yards further along.

6. Turn left onto the bridleway which takes you across fields with views of Redlands Heights to your right. As the field ends, turn right and continue straight ahead, through a barrier, on a signposted public footpath. Keep the hedge on your left and follow it when it turns left and shortly right again. Stay on this path for about half a mile. You will pass a wartime pillbox on your left and then go through some metal posts. The river Mole is now on your left and the backs of houses and gardens on your right. At the last house, join a track coming in from the right. Carry on on downhill over a bridge and then turn right on a footpath over a meadow to another bridge. Continue uphill and through a barrier, alongside a house, out onto a road. Turn right and shortly you will come to The Duke's Head on Brockham Green (HN).

7. Turn left and follow the edge of the green towards Brock-ham church which you pass on your right. The path you are now on brings you out to a road. Continue in the same direction past the village school on your left. After about a quarter of a mile you will reach four houses on your left, all called 'Way'.

8. After the last house turn left on a track which leads to a fenced path with a field on your left and backs of houses on your right. Go over a planked bridge by a footpath sign on a tree and turn right along the edge of a field. In the field corner turn left and at the top you will come to a footpath sign. Turn right, continuing on a fenced path with a field on your right and woods on your left. Your path turns left again at footpath and warning signs and you continue along this enclosed path until you reach a stile on your left.

9. Cross the stile into a field and go forward along the top of a hill where you will have good views of the River Mole and beyond to your left. Later there will be a fence on your left and you continue to a stile leading you downhill through a wooded area to another stile. Follow the path uphill through brambles and into a field, still with the river to your left, head for a brick bridge and finally you will reach a road.

10. Turn left over the bridge and continue past Betchworth House on your left until you reach the entrance to Betchworth church. Turn right along a road by The Dolphin remaining on it for about half a mile. The river Mole is now on your right and to the left there is a signposted footpath, parallel with the road, which can be used for part of the way. Ignore a turning on the left (Sandy Lane) and continue past More Place until you reach the grounds of Wonham Manor on the right.

11. Just past the lodge of Wonham Manor turn left uphill into woods. When the path divides take the left, higher fork. The paths then meet again and you go through a gate to an enclosed footpath at the edge of the field that you crossed earlier in the walk. You will then come to a stile on your right.

12. Cross over the stile and follow the side of a field, with a hedge on your left at first, until you come to a kissing gate. Keep in the same direction, now with a fence on your right. The path takes you uphill towards some trees. Go through another kissing gate and continue ahead passing a house (Juniper Cottage) on your right to reach Dungate's Lane which you walked along earlier.

13. Turn right, back through Dungate's Farm, through woods and over Shag Brook to a gate. Here you should continue forward across a field leading you to another gate where you join an enclosed bridleway. This takes you to Reigate Heath golf course. Cross the green, climb the hill and make for the windmill and clubhouse which you keep on your right. (At the top of the hill there are seats where you may rest and enjoy the view.)

14. Continue past the windmill looking for a trig point on your left, after which bear right with the path. Once past a cottage on your right, go downhill a few paces then turn left on a bridleway which later descends over a green. After passing some trees it goes over another green and leads you through some posts to a car park and the road. Maintain your direction along the road and it is then only a short distance back to The Black Horse.

Historical Notes

Reigate Heath embraces a cricket ground and a golf course. The windmill is not working but is used as a church. Between May and October services are held there on the third Sunday of each month at 3 p.m.

Buckland, as its name suggests, was associated with deer as this was an area where they once abounded, especially the more rare red deer which were preserved here. Buckland Church of Our Lady was rebuilt in 1860 and is noted for its 14th century window which is a fine example of medieval glasswork. The village green is picturesque with its pond, old school house and tithe barn shaped exactly like a church.

Brockham is a name usually associated with badgers which used to abound near the river but it may equally well denote simply 'settlement by a brook'. The green, now the site of Surrey's largest Guy Fawkes' bonfire, was in earlier times an important centre for cricket and players of the calibre of W. G. Grace are known to have played there. The home players wore straw hats manufactured by the village rush-chair maker. Brockham became an ecclesiastical parish, separate from St Michael's, Betchworth, in 1848.

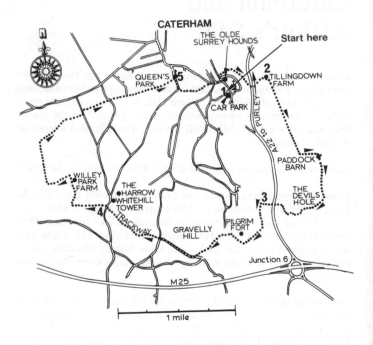

CATERHAM

THE OLDE
SURREY HOUNDS

Start here

QUEEN'S
PARK

5

2

TILLINGDOWN
FARM

1

CAR PARK

PADDOCK
BARN

WILLEY
PARK
FARM

THE
HARROW
WHITEHILL
TOWER

4

TRACKWAY

3

GRAVELLY
HILL

PILGRIM
FORT

THE
DEVILS
HOLE

A22 to PURLEY

Junction 6

M25

1 mile

Caterham and Arthur's Seat

Introduction: This easy walk takes you along field paths and then through very attractive wooded areas following the North Downs Way over Gravelly Hill and White Hill. It is a particularly good walk for the fine views you will have along much of the route. You will pass a folly, Whitehill Tower, which is also known as Arthur's Seat.

Distance: This walk is a 7½-mile circuit and will take 3–3½ hours.

Refreshments: There is only one possibility during the walk. At Point 4 you are very close to The Harrow inn which serves hot and cold bar snacks, Mondays to Saturdays. In Caterham itself there are, of course, several choices, including The Pizza Hut which is close to the car park. The Olde Surrey Hounds, which you pass at the end of the walk, serves bar meals every day except Sundays.

How to get there: The walk commences from the car park near the centre of Caterham. This is not the car park behind the station, shared by BR and Waitrose, but the one off Church Path, a turning off the roundabout. There is a half-hourly train service to Caterham on weekdays. On Sundays they run hourly. There are several bus routes passing through Caterham. (OS maps 187 or TQ 25/35, GR 337554.)

The Walk:
1. Leave the car park, turn left down Church Walk and cross over towards The Olde Surrey Hounds which you pass on your right. Take the second turning right, Mount Pleasant Road, and at the top continue direction on a footpath which soon bears

right and from where you have good views across Caterham. Later your path curves towards a road, the A22, which you cross to some steps opposite leading up to a farm drive. Turn left uphill towards Tillingdown Farm and then turn right at a public footpath sign.

2.   Almost immediately, at another footpath sign, turn right again. You will now be walking for nearly a mile on a long, straight path which here and there affords good views to the left and right. On reaching a fence, at Paddock Barn, turn left along a field. At the end of the farm buildings turn right at a public footpath sign. Go through some metal bars and a gate, then walk down the side of a field, with a hedge on your right, making for a stile in the fence ahead. Once over the stile turn right into woods, continuing with a wire fence on your right and you will find excellent views over to your left. Eventually you go over a bar stile into more woods, then steeply downhill into The Devil's Hole, through the remains of a kissing gate and down some steps. By now the roar of the traffic on the M25 will be apparent. A further set of steps will lead you out on a drive which you cross following the direction of a North Downs Way sign. You go down some more steps, probably noticing a commercial area over on your right, then you cross the drive again, continuing on the North Downs Way. At the next 'NDW' sign, by a stile, turn right up a track for about 100 yards then left over another stile. Cross a field leading to a bridge which takes you back over the A22.

3.   Bear right to a road then turn left uphill. In a short while turn left onto the North Downs Way passing a caravan site on your left, later passing close to the Pilgrims' Fort above you on the right. Where the path forks at a concrete post, bear right uphill. Later on, fork left to cross a green at Gravelly Hill where there are excellent views southwards across the M25 with the South Downs on the horizon. Continue left along the NDW on this fine ridge path and at a fork bear right by an acorn sign. At the next fork go left, soon passing through some green posts. Your route now takes you over a stile and on to War Coppice Road where you proceed uphill for just over half a mile. At the top you will find a folly, Arthur's Seat (HN) on your right and you will come to a road junction.

4.   (If you wish to visit The Harrow inn turn right for about 100 yards.) To continue the walk cross the road and go through the entrance to Willey Park Farm. Turn left immediately onto a

public bridleway over White Hill. At the end of a field your path turns right and leads through a gate towards the farm buildings. Having passed the last building turn left on a bridleway for about a quarter of a mile. When you reach a 'NDW' sign turn right to walk along the side of a field and onto an enclosed path. After passing some farm buildings on your right turn right on a lane signposted to Caterham. At the end turn left then almost immediately right along a pleasant residential road called The Heath. Cross Roffes Lane to a barrier and footpath opposite. Later your route proceeds along a road to another enclosed footpath then goes through a barrier into Queens Park. After passing some tennis courts on your left take an enclosed path leading out to a road.

5.   Turn right and in a short while you will pass the ancient parish church of St Lawrence (HN) on your right and newer church of St Mary's (HN) on your left. Continue downhill on the road back into Caterham (HN). Pass the station on your left and turn right at a roundabout for the car park.

Historical Notes

Whitehill Tower, also known as Arthur's Seat was built in the late 18th-century of flint faced with stone. It is uncertain who built this folly, but it certainly would have given him commanding views over the North Downs and, no doubt, the South Downs beyond. To the north-east he would also have had an excellent view of the City of London on a clear day.

St Lawrence Church is the old parish church of Caterham and dates from Norman times. It was built in 1095, enlarged in 1200 and a north aisle added in 1230. This church became too small for a town the size of Caterham and was disused from 1866 until 1927 when it was reopened. Some services are still held there today.

St Mary's Church, was built in 1866, to replace its neighbour opposite.

Caterham is a town with some traces of the old village and is now the administrative centre of Tandridge Council, created in the local government reorganisation of 1974 from a merger of Caterham and Warlingham Urban District and Godstone Rural District Councils. Caterham is comprised of two places, Caterham-on-the-Hill and Caterham Valley. Some will remember the former with less than affection, having passed through as Coldstream Guardsmen. The Guards depot was built in 1877 along with St Lawrence's Hospital and they were the forerunners of this now busy community. Caterham Valley grew up when the railway arrived in 1856.

Oxted, The Pilgrims Way and Limpsfield

Introduction: This fairly easy walk takes you through woods and fields and over chalk downland noted for its wild flowers. It also has plenty to offer those interested in history as there is much evidence of Roman activity in the area and you will pass two very old churches on the route. One long but gradual climb up to the Pilgrims Way is made worthwhile for the panoramic views from the top.

Distance: The walk is a 7-mile circuit and will take approximately 3–3½ hours.

Refreshments: There are plenty of shops in Oxted and one or two in Limpsfield. At the start of the walk, close to the station, is Hoskins Hotel. Old Oxted, which is nearby, has several delightful pubs including The Old Bell Tavern which is 15th century and, besides being one of the best-known watering holes in East Surrey, is the oldest and most attractive building in the village. In Limpsfield you will pass a pleasant inn called The Bell.

How to get there: The walk commences from the large car park on the up-line side of Oxted Station, for which you have to pay, but there is an adjacent free car park. There is an hourly train service to Oxted station every day including Sundays. There is a bus service to Oxted and an infrequent one to Limpsfield where the walk may be commenced at Point 7. (OS maps 187 or TQ 25/35 & TQ 45/55, GR 393528.)

The Walk:
1.   Leave the car park via a signposted pedestrian exit, passing the station entrance on your right and continue down Station

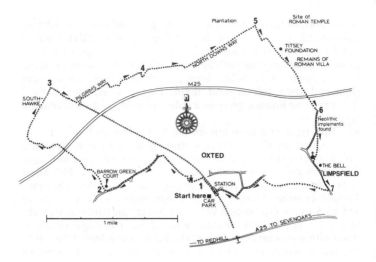

Approach. At a road junction turn left and cross over to St Mary's Church (HN). Go through a gate into the churchyard, passing the church on your right, and leave through the far gate. Ignore a footpath opposite and turn right along a drive then left on an enclosed bridleway. This takes you past a burial ground on your right and continues between fields. On reaching a road turn left, shortly curving left along a road signposted to Godstone. Half a mile further on you will cross a stream and there will be a metal fence and a row of very high conifers on your right. After passing the entrance to Barrow Green Court (HN) you will come to a bridleway.

2. Turn right and later your track takes you onto a bridge over the M25. When you come to a gate at a fork your path is the enclosed one bearing left uphill. In an area of very large, beautiful beech trees the path divides and you veer to the right, still going steadily uphill. At the top bear right through beech woods, stopping at the South Hawke viewpoint to admire the vista across to Oxted and beyond, then continue on over a dip to a North Downs Way sign.

3. Turn right downhill, soon making a steep descent down 85 steps with a strong rail to assist you. (As you come down you may spot the air shaft for Oxted railway tunnel which is beneath you.)

At the bottom turn left over a stile and go along a narrow path on the edge of the hill tracing the old Pilgrims Way (HN). (Watch out for exposed tree roots here.) At an 'NDW' sign turn right downhill following the path to the middle of a field where it turns left at a further sign. When your path reaches some woods bear right and then left around them. Continue across the field towards some houses, go over a stile and shortly you will reach a lane.

4. Turn right and soon left on the North Downs Way. Cross a stile and disregard an immediate turning on the right. Keep going uphill until you reach another stile on the right, with an acorn sign, which you cross. Continue along the contour of the hill, soon with a fence on your right. Cross a stile and follow the path to another stile. Here there is a sign indicating that you are at Link 5 to the Greensand Way, but you should continue straight ahead on the North Downs Way along the edge of three fields with a plantation on your left. Each field is linked by a stile the last of which will take you to some steps down to a rough lane.

5. Turn right downhill and at the bottom go over a track coming in from the right up to some steps marked with a Titsey Foundation Walk sign. Go over a stile onto an enclosed path round a field and then over another stile, down some steps, to a lane on which turn right. When the lane curves right, at the entrance to the Titsey Foundation (HN) car park, continue forward on a bridleway through the woods, through a tunnel under the motorway, out to a road.

6. Turn right along the road (with great care and in single file) and at the top of a slope cross over to a 30 MPH sign and turn onto a public footpath. (If this is badly overgrown continue up the road for a short way and turn left onto a driveway and soon bear right towards a churchyard.) This enclosed path will eventually lead across a driveway and on through St Peter's (HN) churchyard where you pass the church on your right. Leave the churchyard through a lychgate and continue left down Limpsfield (HN) High Street. You will pass Detillens on your right and The Bull inn on your left. Immediately after passing the Post Office on the right you will find a public footpath sign near the entrance to Priest Hill.

7. Turn right along this path which takes you through a kissing gate into a new housing estate. Continue down through the estate and out to a main road. Turn left for about 50 yards and then right onto a narrow, enclosed footpath. Go over a stile into a field following an obvious track to the other side where you go through a kissing gate. Soon you cross the river Eden onto another enclosed footpath which leads you to a road on which turn left passing some attractive houses. At a junction turn left and at the next junction at Woolworths turn right up Station Road East. Take the next turning left and go through Oxted Station subway to the car park.

Historical Notes

Oxted still retains some of its old village charm but all around there has been development. The A25 divides Old Oxted from the relatively newer part, developed mainly during the early part of this century and, of course, the new M25 motorway runs close by. Master Park, in the centre of the town, was a gift from Charles Hoskins Master, lord of the manor, who in 1923 decreed that the greater part of Marls Field, as it was originally known, was to be 'laid out and preserved for ever thereafter for the healthy recreation and amusement of the inhabitants of the parish of Oxted and their friends'.

St Mary's Church is medieval but restored. It has a 12th century tower of dark Bargate stone. Interesting features are the 13th century priest's doorway in the chancel, an old iron chest, probably 15th century, and stained glass in the lights of the east window, probably 14th century.

Barrow Green Court is a 17th century manor house and was once the home of the historian Grote. It is now owned by a wealthy gentleman from the Middle East who has turned it into something of a fortress.

The Pilgrims Way can be traced near here. On an 18th century map this track is marked as the old way from Titsey to Limpsfield. Nearby is the site of a Roman villa and Roman road and it is thought that the east–west terraceway below the chalk escarpment was used by the Romans.

Titsey Foundation comprises a park in a heavily wooded area. The grounds are open to the public, as eventually will be the house which was once the home of the Gresham family. Sir John Gresham pulled down the manor house in 1775 and rebuilt on the same site. The church, which was a matter of a few feet from the house, was removed then rebuilt on its present site on the other side of the road. The park passed from the Greshams to the Leveson Gower family through marriage, and one of their number was responsible for discovering a Roman villa in the grounds in 1864.

St Peter's Church has been described as 'a dour piece of Wealden building' and has a 14th century lychgate. The tower dates from about 1180. The nave, chancel and south side are restored 13th century work. Curious recesses behind the altar were possibly used for the baking of Communion bread. The grave of Frederick Delius, the great composer, is in the beautiful churchyard to the north. He was buried in France but his remains were moved here in 1935 as he had often expressed a wish to be buried in an English village.

Limpsfield High Street contains some very picturesque half-timbered houses and cottages. Detillens is a 15th-century hall with a kingpost roof and early 18th century road frontage and is open April–September. Limpsfield was mentioned in the Domesday Book as being held by the Abbot of Battle. William the Conqueror's surveyors found, among other things, a mill, fishery and church, two stone quarries, and three hawks' nests in the woodland.